Lowercase Letters

a b c d e f g h i j k l

m n o p q r s t u v w x

y z 1 2 3 4 5 6 7 8 9

a b c d e f g h i j k l

m n o p q r s t u v w x

y z 1 2 3 4 5 6 7 8 9

a b c d e f g h i j k l

m n o p q r s t u v w x

y z 1 2 3 4 5 6 7 8 9

Capital Letters

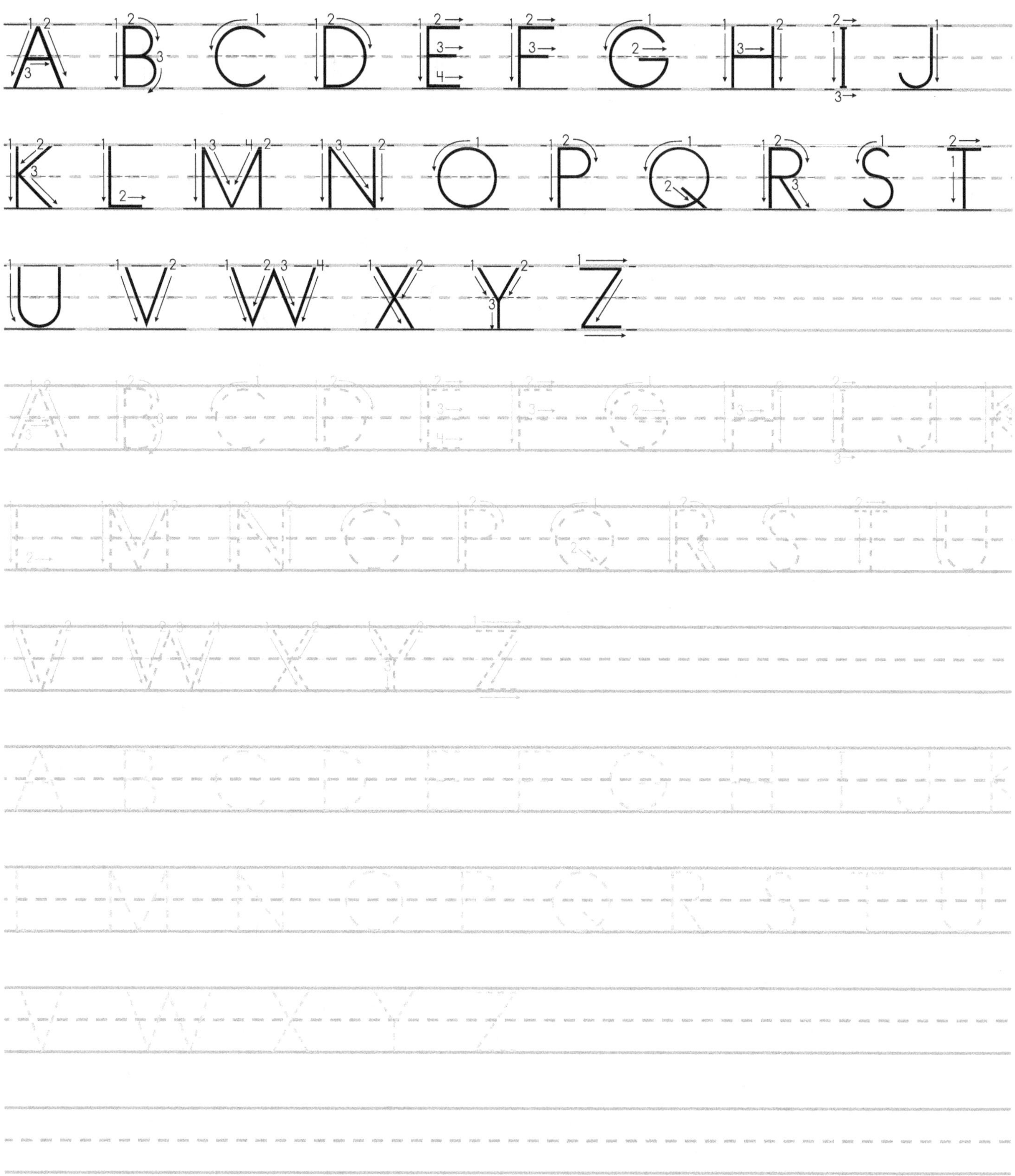

Practice each print letter, then write your own.

b b b b b b b
b b b b b b b b
b b b b b b b b

B B B B B B B
B B B B B B B
B B B B B B B

Practice each print letter, then write your own.

a a a a a a a

a a a a a a a

A A A A A A A A

Practice each print letter, then write your own.

Practice each print letter, then write your own.

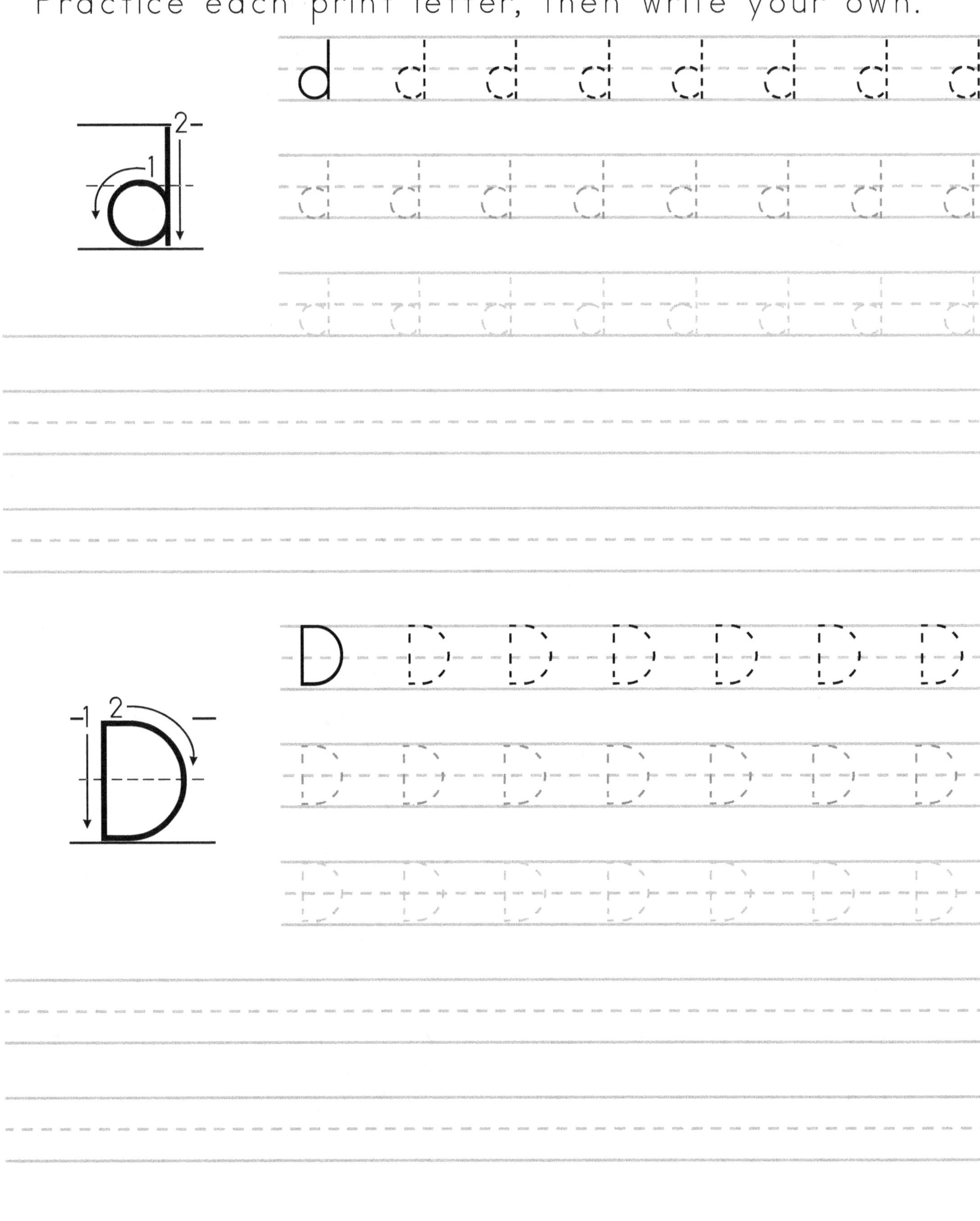

Practice each print letter, then write your own.

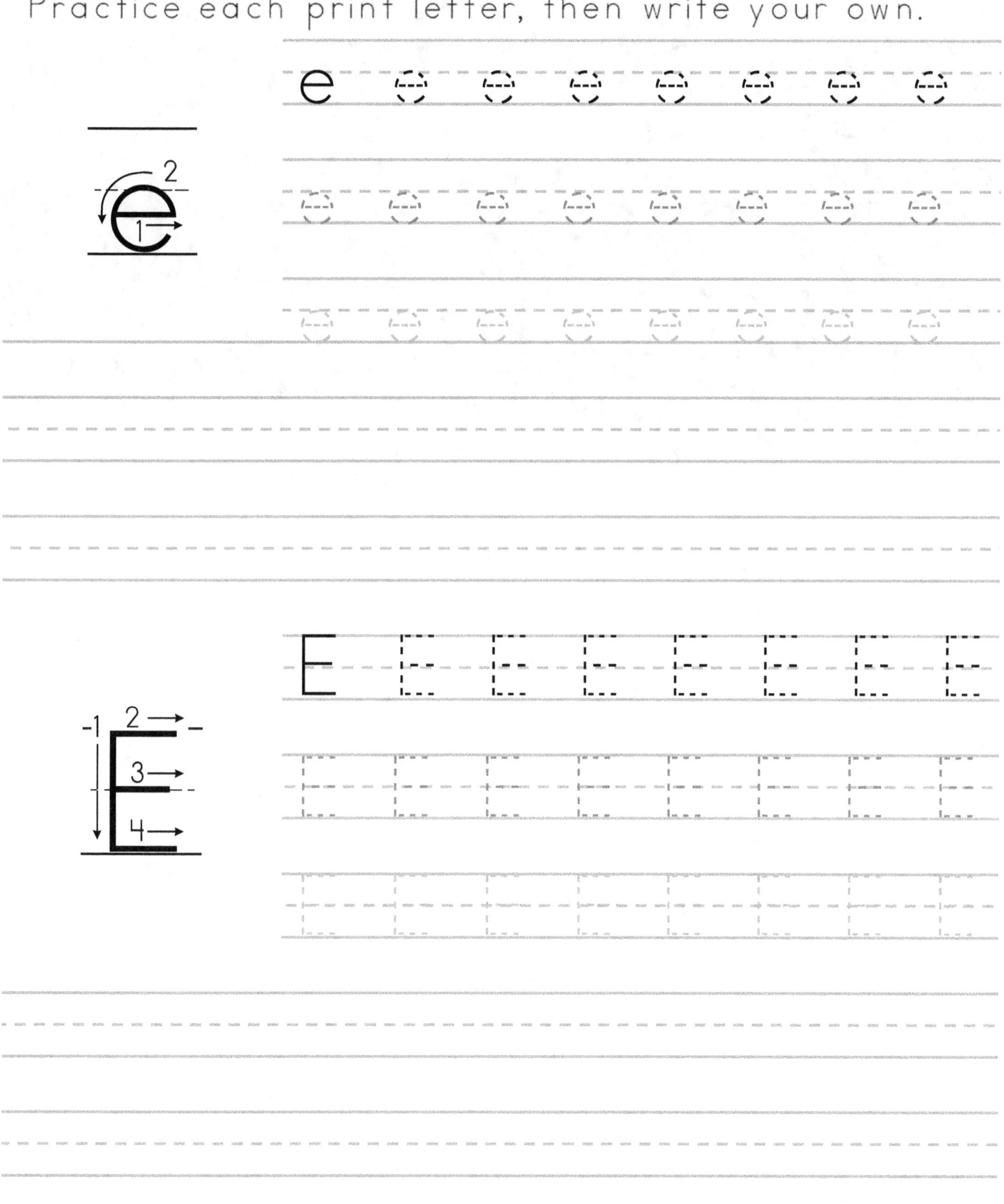

Practice each print letter, then write your own.

Practice each print letter, then write your own.

g g g g g g g

g g g g g g g g

g

Practice each print letter, then write your own.

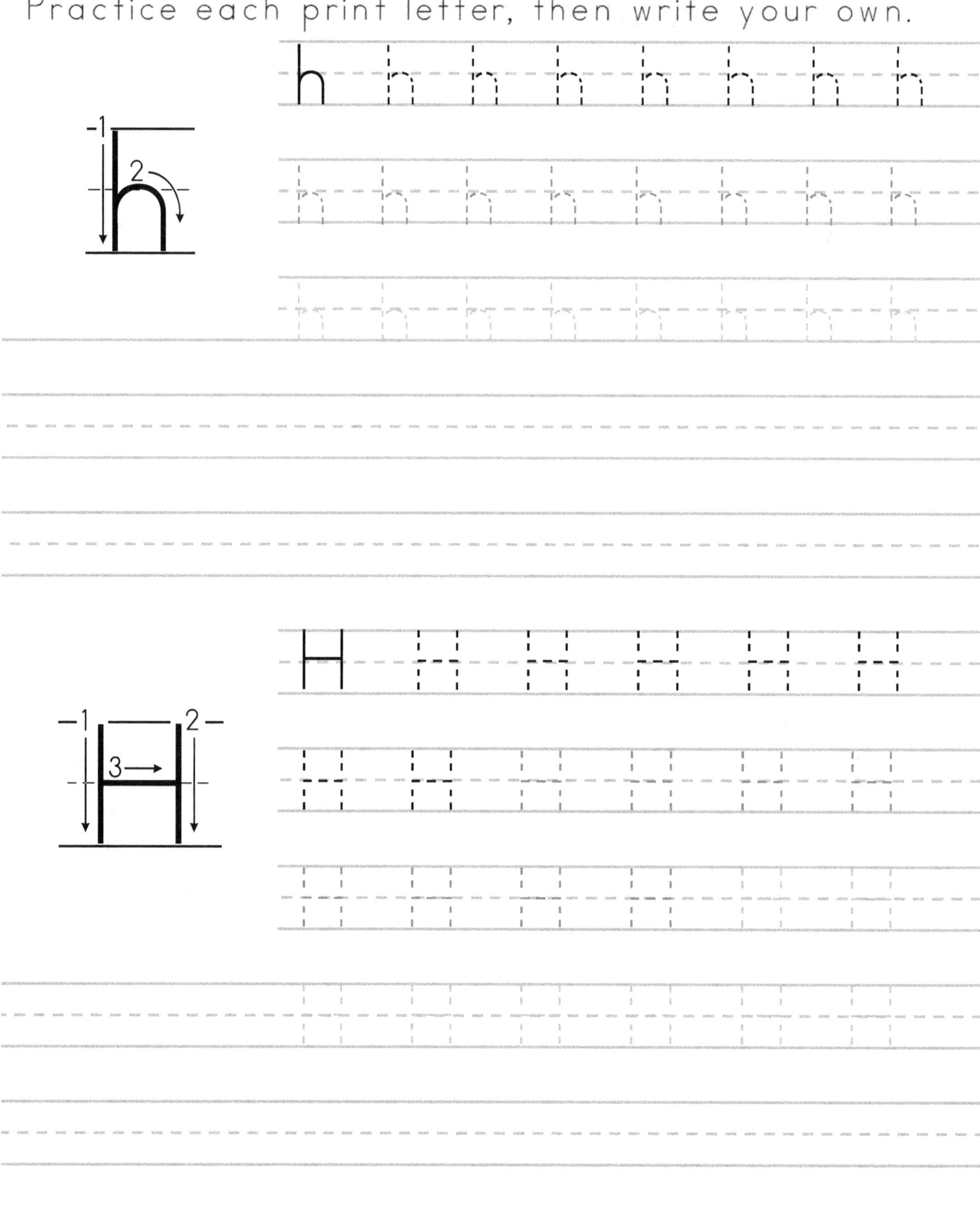

Practice each print letter, then write your own.

Practice each print letter, then write your own.

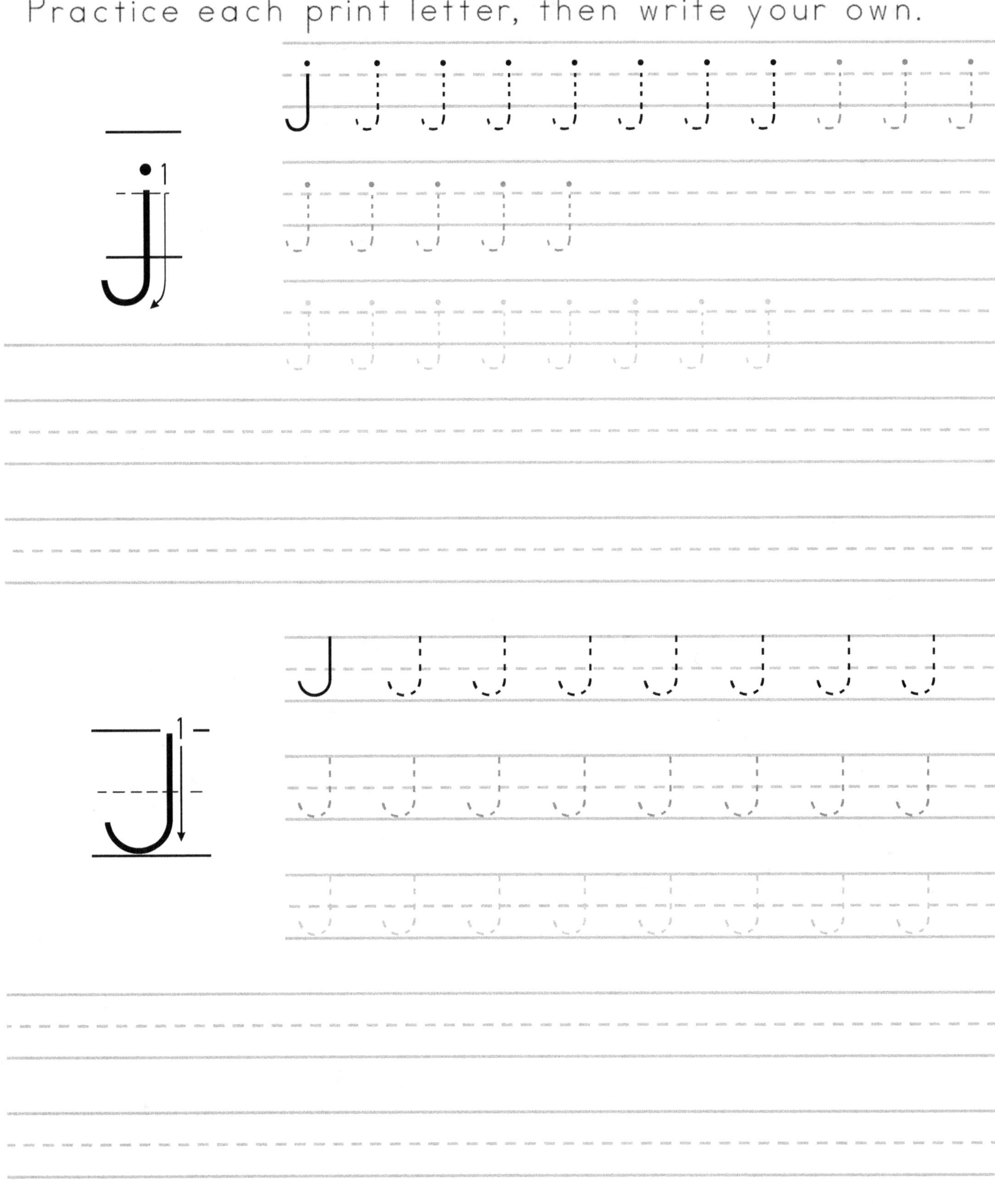

Practice each print letter, then write your own.

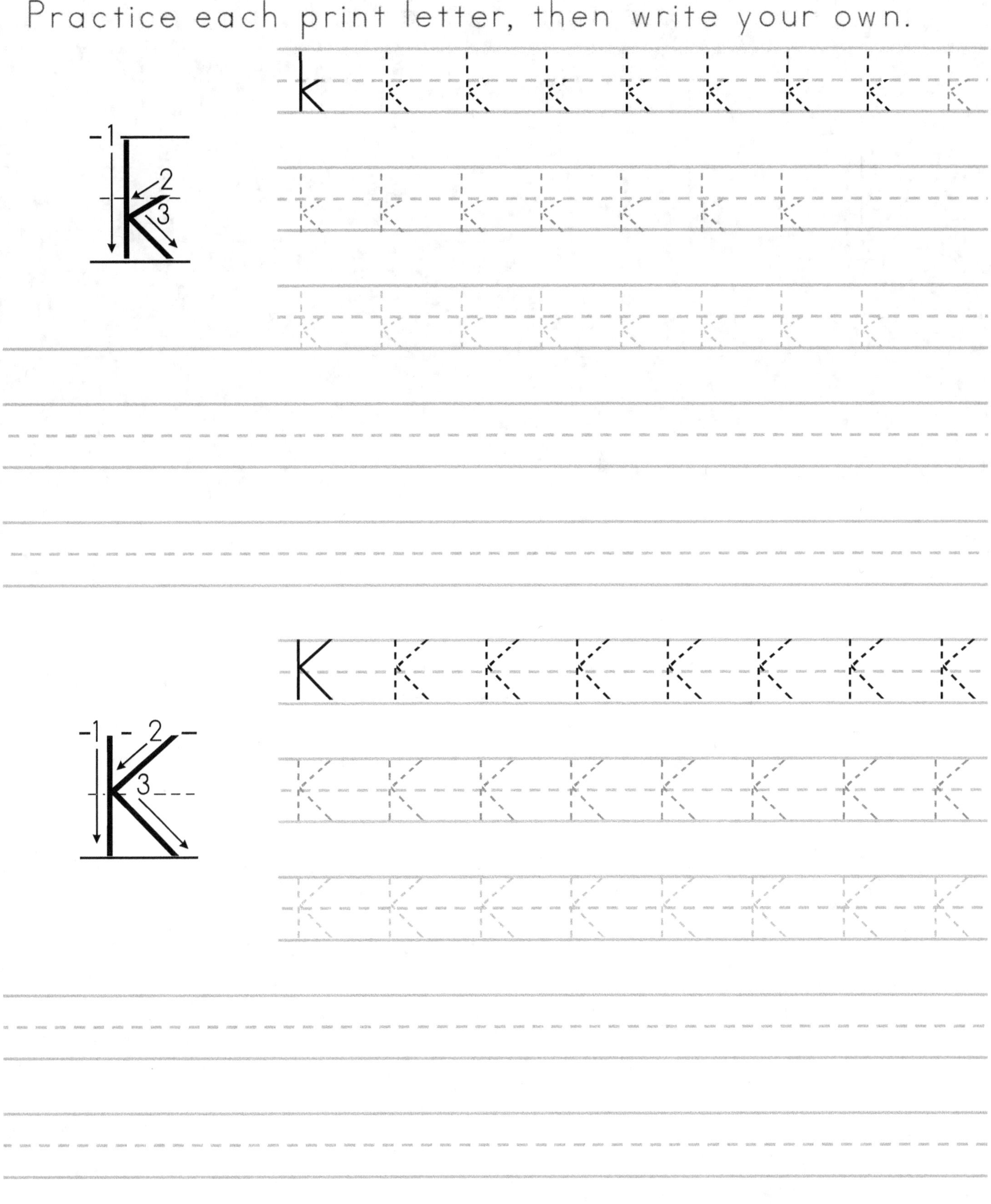

Practice each print letter, then write your own.

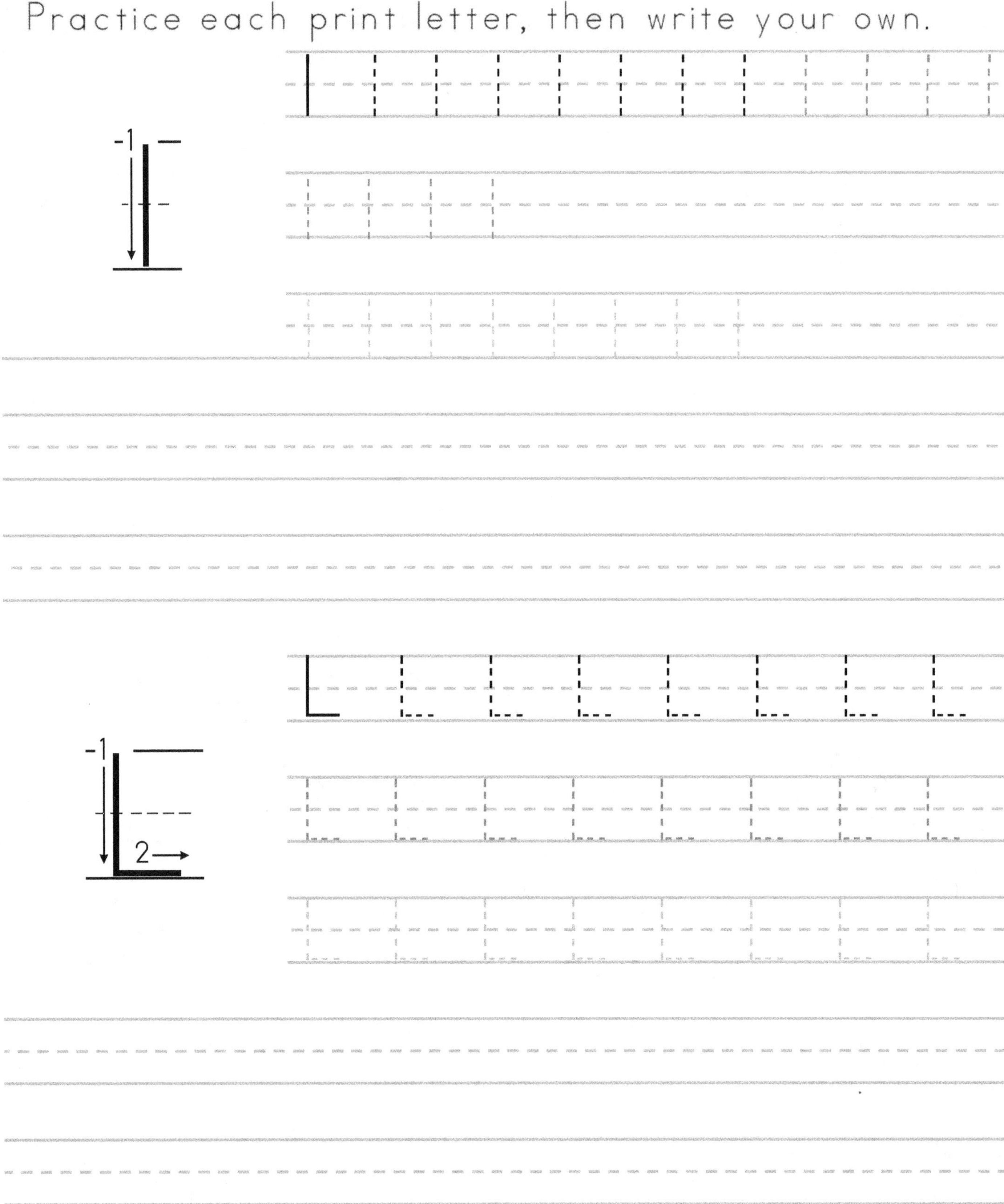

Practice each print letter, then write your own.

Practice each print letter, then write your own.

Practice each print letter, then write your own.

Practice each print letter, then write your own.

Practice each print letter, then write your own.

Practice each print letter, then write your own.

Practice each print letter, then write your own.

Practice each print letter, then write your own.

Practice each print letter, then write your own.

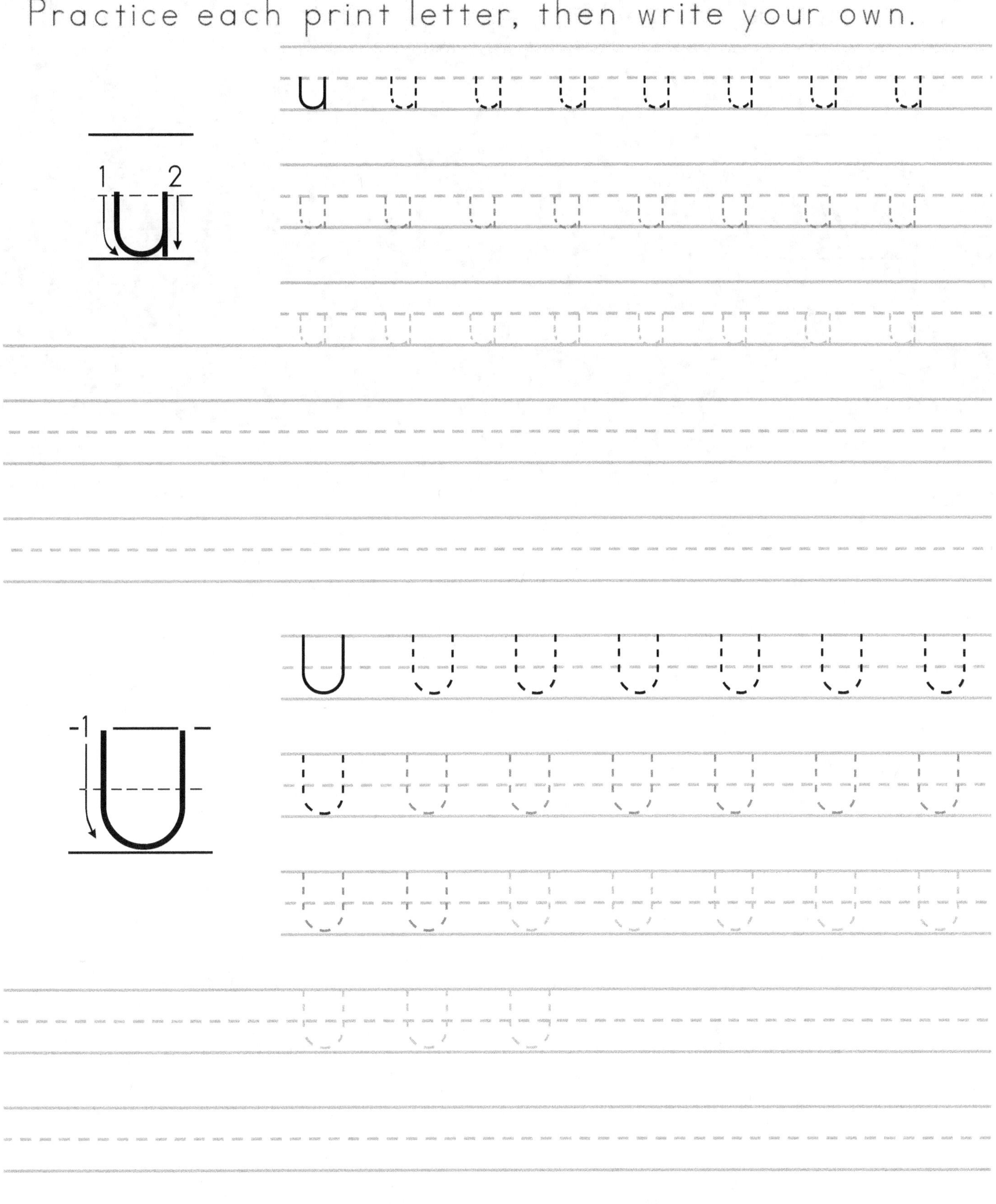

Practice each print letter, then write your own.

Practice each print letter, then write your own.

W W W W W W W W

w w w w w w w w

1 2 3 4

W W W W W

w w w w w

Practice each print letter, then write your own.

Practice each print letter, then write your own.

Practice each print letter, then write your own.

39 Books of the Old Testament

Genesis Exodus
Leviticus Numbers
Deuteronomy Joshua
Judges Ruth 1 Samuel
2 Samuel 1 Kings
2 Kings 1 Chronicles
2 Chronicles Ezra
Nehemiah Esther
Job Psalms Proverbs
Ecclesiastes
Song of Songs Isaiah

Books of the Old Testament (continued)

Jeremiah Lamentations
Ezekiel   Daniel
Hosea   Joel
Amos   Obadiah
Jonah   Micah
Nahum   Habakkuk
Zephaniah   Haggai
Zechariah   Malachi

39 Books of the Old
Testament

Genesis   Exodus
Leviticus   Numbers
Deuteronomy Joshua
Judges Ruth 1 Samuel
2 Samuel   1 Kings
2 Kings   1 Chronicles
2 Chronicles   Ezra
Nehemiah   Esther
Job Psalms Proverbs
Ecclesiastes
Song of Songs Isaiah

Books of the Old Testament (continued)

Jeremiah Lamentations
Ezekiel   Daniel
Hosea   Joel
Amos   Obadiah
Jonah   Micah
Nahum   Habakkuk
Zephaniah   Haggai
Zechariah   Malachi

39 Books of the Old Testament

Genesis   Exodus
Leviticus   Numbers
Deuteronomy   Joshua
Judges   Ruth   1 Samuel
2 Samuel   1 Kings
2 Kings   1 Chronicles
2 Chronicles   Ezra
Nehemiah   Esther
Job   Psalms   Proverbs
Ecclesiastes
Song of Songs   Isaiah

Books of the Old
Testament (Continued)

Jeremiah Lamentations
Ezekiel Daniel
Hosea Joel
Amos Obadiah
Jonah Micah
Nahum Habakkuk
Zephaniah Haggai
Zechariah Malachi

27 Books New Testament
Matthew Mark Luke
John   Acts   Romans
1 Corinthians
2 Corinthians Galatians
Ephesians Philippians
Colossians
1 Thessalonians
2 Thessalonians
1 Timothy 2 Timothy
Titus   Philemon Hebrews
James 1 Peter 2 Peter
1 John 2 John 3 John
Jude Revelation

27 Books New Testament
Matthew Mark Luke
John   Acts Romans
1 Corinthians
2 Corinthians Galatians
Ephesians Philippians
Colossians
1 Thessalonians
2 Thessalonians
1 Timothy 2 Timothy
Titus Philemon Hebrews
James 1 Peter 2 Peter
1 John 2 John 3 John
Jude Revelation

27 Books New Testament

Matthew Mark Luke

John Acts Romans

1 Corinthians

2 Corinthians Galatians

Ephesians Philippians

Colossians

1 Thessalonians

2 Thessalonians

1 Timothy 2 Timothy

Titus Philemon Hebrews

James 1 Peter 2 Peter

1 John 2 John 3 John

Jude Revelation

In the beginning God
created the heavens
and the earth.
Genesis 1:1

In the beginning God
created the heavens
and the earth.
Genesis 1:1

For God so loved the
world that he gave his
one and only Son,
that whoever believes
in him shall not perish
but have eternal life.
John 3:16

For God so loved the
world that he gave his
one and only Son,
that whoever believes
in him shall not perish
but have eternal life.
John 3:16

For God so loved the
world that he gave his
one and only Son,
that whoever believes
in him shall not perish
but have eternal life.
John 3:16

"For I know the plans I have for you," declares the LORD, "plans to prosper you and not to harm you, plans to give you hope and a future." Jeremiah 29:11

"For I know the plans I have for you," declares the LORD, "plans to prosper you and not to harm you, plans to give you hope and a future." Jeremiah 29:11

"For I know the plans I
have for you," declares
the LORD, "plans to
prosper you and not to
harm you, plans to give
you hope and a
future." Jeremiah 29:11

And we know that in all things God works for the good of those who love him, who have been called according to his purpose. Romans 8:28

And we know that in all things God works for the good of those who love him, who have been called according to his purpose. Romans 8:28

And we know that in all things God works for the good of those who love him, who have been called according to this purpose. Romans 8:28

I can do everything
through him who gives
me strength.
Philippians 4:13
I can do everything
through him who gives
me strength.
Philippians 4:13

Trust in the LORD with all your heart and lean not on your own understanding. Proverbs 3:5

Trust in the LORD with all your heart and lean not on your own understanding. Proverbs 3:5

Do not conform any longer to the pattern of this world, but be transformed by the renewing of your mind. Then you will be able to test and approve what God's will is.
Romans 12:2

Do not conform any
longer to the pattern of
this world, but be
transformed by the
renewing of your mind.
Then you will be able to
test and approve what
God's will is.
Romans 12:2

Do not be anxious
about anything, but in
everything, by prayer
and petition, with
thanksgiving, present
your requests to God.
Philippians 4:6
Do not be anxious
about anything, but in
everything, by prayer
and petition, with
thanksgiving, present
your requests to God.
Philippians 4:6

Therefore go and make disciples of all nations, baptizing them in the name of the Father and of the Son and of the Holy Spirit. Matthew 28:19

Therefore go and make disciples of all nations, baptizing them in the name of the Father and of the Son and of the Holy Spirit. Matthew 28:19

For it is by grace you have been saved, through faith—and this not from yourselves, it is the gift of God. Ephesians 2:8

For it is by grace you have been saved, through faith—and this not from yourselves, it is the gift of God. Ephesians 2:8

But the fruit of the
Spirit is love, joy, peace,
forbearance, kindness,
goodness, faithfulness,
gentleness and self-
control. Against such
things there is no law.
Galatians 5:22-23

But the fruit of the
Spirit is love, joy, peace,
forbearance, kindness,
goodness, faithfulness,
gentleness and self-
control. Against such
things there is no law.
Galatians 5:22-23

Therefore, I urge you,
brothers, in view of
God's mercy, to offer
your bodies as living
sacrifices, holy and
pleasing to God—this is
your spiritual act of
worship.
Romans 12:1

Therefore, I urge you, brothers, in view of God's mercy, to offer your bodies as living sacrifices, holy and pleasing to God—this is your spiritual act of worship.
Romans 12:1

The thief comes only to
steal and kill and
destroy; I have come
that they may have
life, and have it to the
full. John 10:10

The thief comes only to
steal and kill and
destroy; I have come
that they may have
life, and have it to the
full. John 10:10

For I am with you, and
no one is going to
attack and harm you,
because I have many
people in this city."
Acts 18:10

For I am with you, and
no one is going to
attack and harm you,
because I have many
people in this city."
Acts 18:10

One night the Lord
spoke to Paul in a
vision: "Do not be
afraid; keep on
speaking, do not be
silent. Acts 18:9

One night the Lord
spoke to Paul in a
vision: "Do not be
afraid; keep on
speaking, do not be
silent. Acts 18:9

One night the Lord spoke to Paul in a vision: "Do not be afraid; keep on speaking, do not be silent. Acts 18:9

One night the Lord spoke to Paul in a vision: "Do not be afraid; keep on speaking, do not be silent. Acts 18:9

So Paul stayed for a
year and a half,
teaching them the word
of God. Acts 18:11

So Paul stayed for a
year and a half,
teaching them the word
of God. Acts 18:11

I have been crucified
with Christ and I no
longer live, but Christ
lives in me. The life I
live in the body, I live
by faith in the Son of
God, who loved me and
gave himself for me.
Galatians 2:20.

I have been crucified
with Christ and I no
longer live, but Christ
lives in me. The life I
live in the body, I live
by faith in the Son of
God, who loved me and
gave himself for me.
Galatians 2:20.

If we confess our sins,
he is faithful and just
and will forgive us our
sins and purify us from
all unrighteousness.
1 John 1:9

If we confess our sins,
he is faithful and just
and will forgive us our
sins and purify us from
all unrighteousness.
1 John 1:9

For all have sinned and
fall short of the glory
of God.
Romans 3:23

For all have sinned and
fall short of the glory
of God.
Romans 3:23

Jesus answered, "I am the way and the truth and the life. No one comes to the Father except through me. John 14:6

Jesus answered, "I am the way and the truth and the life. No one comes to the Father except through me. John 14:6

And teaching them to
obey everything I have
commanded you. And
surely I am with you
always, to the very end
of the age.
Matthew 28:20

And teaching them to
obey everything I have
commanded you. And
surely I am with you
always, to the very end
of the age.
Matthew 28:20

But God demonstrates his own love for us in this: While we were still sinners, Christ died for us. Romans 5:8

But God demonstrates his own love for us in this: While we were still sinners, Christ died for us. Romans 5:8

Finally, brothers, whatever is true, whatever is noble, whatever is right, whatever is pure, whatever is lovely, whatever is admirable—if anything is excellent or praiseworthy—think about such things. Philippians 4:8

And the peace of God, which transcends all understanding, will guard your hearts and your minds in Christ Jesus.. Philippians 4:7

And the peace of God, which transcends all understanding, will guard your hearts and your minds in Christ Jesus.. Philippians 4:7

Have I not commanded you? Be strong and courageous. Do not be terrified; do not be discouraged, for the LORD your God will be with you wherever you go." Joshua 1:9

But those who hope in the LORD will renew their strength. They will soar on wings like eagles; they will run and not grow weary, they will walk and not be faint. Isaiah 40:31

For it is by grace you
have been saved,
through faith—and this
is not from yourselves,
it is the gift of God—
9 not by works, so that
no one can boast.
Ephesians 2:8-9

For the wages of sin is death, but the gift of God is eternal life in Christ Jesus our Lord. Romans 6:23

For the wages of sin is death, but the gift of God is eternal life in Christ Jesus our Lord. Romans 6:23

But he was pierced for our transgressions, he was crushed for our iniquities; the punishment that brought us peace was upon him, and by his wounds we are healed. Isaiah 53:5

But in your hearts set apart Christ as Lord. Always be prepared to give an answer to everyone who asks you to give the reason for the hope that you have. But do this with gentleness and respect. 1 Peter 3:15

All Scripture is God-breathed and is useful for teaching, rebuking, correcting and training in righteousness.
2 Timothy 3:16

All Scripture is God-breathed and is useful for teaching, rebuking, correcting and training in righteousness.
2 Timothy 3:16

But seek first his kingdom and his righteousness, and all these things will be given to you as well. Matthew 6:33

But seek first his kingdom and his righteousness, and all these things will be given to you as well. Matthew 6:33

Let us fix our eyes on Jesus, the author and perfecter of our faith, who for the joy set before him endured the cross, scorning its shame, and sat down at the right hand of the throne of God. Hebrews 12:2

Cast all your anxiety
on him because he
cares for you.
1 Peter 5:7

Cast all your anxiety
on him because he
cares for you.
1 Peter 5:7

For we are God's workmanship, created in Christ Jesus to do good works, which God prepared in advance for us to do. Ephesians 2:10

For we are God's workmanship, created in Christ Jesus to do good works, which God prepared in advance for us to do. Ephesians 2:10

No temptation has
seized you except what
is common to man. And
God is faithful; he will
not let you be tempted
beyond what you can
bear. But when you are
tempted, he will also
provide a way out so
that you can stand up
under it.
1 Corinthians 10:13

Come to me, all you
who are weary and
burdened, and I will
give you rest.
Matthew 11:28

Come to me, all you
who are weary and
burdened, and I will
give you rest.
Matthew 11:28

Now faith is being sure
of what we hope for
and certain of what we
do not see. Hebrews 11:1

Now faith is being sure
of what we hope for
and certain of what we
do not see. Hebrews 11:1

Therefore, if anyone is in Christ, he is a new creation; the old has gone, the new has come! 2 Corinthians 5:17

Therefore, if anyone is in Christ, he is a new creation; the old has gone, the new has come! 2 Corinthians 5:17

Keep your lives free from the love of money and be content with what you have, because God has said, "Never will I leave you; never will I forsake you." Hebrews 13:5

But he said to me, "My grace is sufficient for you, for my power is made perfect in weakness." Therefore I will boast all the more gladly about my weaknesses, so that Christ's power may rest on me.
2 Corinthians 12:9

That if you confess with your mouth, "Jesus is Lord," and believe in your heart that God raised him from the dead, you will be saved. Romans 10:9

That if you confess with your mouth, "Jesus is Lord," and believe in your heart that God raised him from the dead, you will be saved. Romans 10:9

So do not fear, for I am with you; do not be dismayed, for I am your God. I will strengthen you and help you; I will uphold you with my righteous right hand. Isaiah 41:10

Then God said, "Let us make man in our image, in our likeness, and let them rule over the fish of the sea and the birds of the air, over the livestock, over all the earth, and over all the creatures that move along the ground." Genesis 1:26

Then God said, "Let us
make man in our image,
in our likeness, and let
them rule over the fish
of the sea and the
birds of the air, over
the livestock, over all
the earth, and over all
the creatures that move
along the ground."
Genesis 1:26

Take my yoke upon you
and learn from me, for
I am gentle and humble
in heart, and you will
find rest for your souls.
Matthew 11:29

"I have told you these things, so that in me you may have peace. In this world you will have trouble. But take heart! I have overcome the world." John 16:33

But you will receive power when the Holy Spirit comes on you; and you will be my witnesses in Jerusalem, and in all Judea and Samaria, and to the ends of the earth. Acts 1:8

For God did not give us a spirit of timidity, but a spirit of power, of love and of self-discipline.
2 Timothy 1:7

Surely, he took up our
infirmities and carried
our sorrows, yet we
considered him stricken
by God, smitten by him,
and afflicted.
Isaiah 53:4

God made him who had no sin to be sin for us, so that in him we might become the righteousness of God. 2 Corinthians 5:21

May the God of hope fill you with all joy and peace as you trust in him, so that you may overflow with hope by the power of the Holy Spirit. Romans 15:13

Jesus said to her, "I am the resurrection and the life. He who believes in me will live, even though he dies. John 11:25

And without faith it is
impossible to please
God, because anyone
who comes to him must
believe that he exists
and that he rewards
those who earnestly seek
him. Hebrews 11:6

I tell you the truth, whoever hears my word and believes him who sent me has eternal life and will not be condemned; he has crossed over from death to life. John 5:24

Consider it pure joy, my brothers, whenever you face trials of many kinds. James 1:2

Consider it pure joy, my brothers, whenever you face trials of many kinds. James 1:2

We all, like sheep, have gone astray, each of us has turned to his own way; and the LORD has laid on him the iniquity of us all. Isaiah 53:6

Peter replied, "Repent
and be baptized, every
one of you, in the name
of Jesus Christ for the
forgiveness of your sins.
And you will receive the
gift of the Holy Spirit."
Acts 2:38

Now to him who is able to do immeasurably more than all we ask or imagine, according to his power that is at work within us. Ephesians 3:20

For my yoke is easy and
my burden is light.
Matthew 11:30

For my yoke is easy and
my burden is light.
Matthew 11:30

So God created man in his own image, in the image of God he created him; male and female he created them. Genesis 1:27

Therefore, as God's chosen people, holy and dearly loved, clothe yourselves with compassion, kindness, humility, gentleness and patience. Colossians 3:12

www.ingramcontent.com/pod-product-compliance
Lightning Source LLC
Chambersburg PA
CBHW081344160726
48000CB00010B/3226